THE LAST LAIRD OF COLL

Mairi Hedderwick was born in Gourock. At twenty she took a job as a mother's help on the Isle of Coll, beginning a life-long love affair with islands and their small communities. Mairi's island world is delightfully reflected in the imaginary island of Struay where her perennially popular Katie Morag stories are set. As well as writing and illustrating children's books Mairi writes and illustrates travel books for adults and the popular series of Hebridean stationery. She lives on Coll.

The Last Laird of Coll

Mairi Hedderwick

BIRLINN

First published in 2011 by
Birlinn Limited
West Newington House
10 Newington Road
Edinburgh
EH9 1QS

www.birlinn.co.uk

ISBN: 978 1 78027 019 7

British Library Cataloguing-in-Publication Data
A catalogue record for this book is available from the
British Library

Typeset by Edderston Book Design, Peebles
Printed and bound in the UK by CPI

Ma 's briag bhuam e, is briag h-ugam e

If it be a lie from me, it is a lie to me

(Gaelic saying)

Contents

Introduction

I first met Kenneth Stewart in 1959. My student job that summer was as *au pair* to his small family. I had never been west of Gourock, on the banks of the Clyde, except for the previous summer when I had gone with a school friend and her family to Tiree, the neighbouring island to Coll. I was captivated by the land, sea, skies and way of life. The boat journey. There was no question when I saw the advertisement for a job on Coll.

I had heard that my employer was the Laird of Coll, so when the *Claymore* dropped anchor in Loch Eatharna I was prepared to be met by a kilted character from *Brigadoon*. Perhaps a deerhound or two. I also knew he had a castle. Which turret would I be sleeping in?

As the ferryboat drew near, there he was steering it alongside. The kilt, of course, but with welly boots and a knitted toorie hat, pipe jutting from his mouth. The ferryman was in fact Guy Jardine, a former Rhodesian farmer and wild colonial boy. Innocently I introduced myself to him as I clambered down in my newly acquired oilskin coat. 'No, girl,' he said, chewing his pipe, 'the Laird is on the jetty waiting for you. I bought the hotel from him.'

Kenneth Stewart was wearing no kilt but workman's trousers, a leather-shouldered donkey jacket and a faded tweed skip bunnet. There were no deerhounds. A black and brown collie dog sat waiting in a rusty battered Land Rover with a flapping canvas hood.

No castle awaited my nervous arrival. There was a little wood-lined bedroom above the kitchen at Acha, a converted schoolhouse at the west end of the island which was the Stewart family home. There was a castle but it was in a very ruinous state. The Laird of Coll was a farmer.

Coll and the Stewart family became part of my student summers and subsequently we lived there with our own family working on the Estate and our croft at Totamore.

I thank them for introducing me to the blessed isle with all its vagaries and moods – in turns joyful, frustrating, celebratory and sometimes painful – all of which they have known only too well.

Kenneth Stewart is now in his mid-eighties and has retired to the Borders, chair-bound but with a very active mind and prodigious memory. A great storyteller. I hope I have done justice to his tales and that his epigrammatic voice with its West Coast inflection can be heard between the lines.

I would also like to thank Robert Sturgeon, the grandson of the famous postmaster, who set up the taping technology and whose wealth of family photographs prompted many of Kenneth's memories, and John McKechnie, who worked for 20 years for the Coll Estate.

Mairi Hedderwick
Isle of Coll, May 2011

The Isle of Coll

~⌒~

The Isle of Coll lies approximately 60 miles west of the Scottish mainland port of Oban and forms part of a group of islands known as the Inner Hebrides. It is roughly thirteen miles long and three miles wide. Shaped like a fish, its head faces northeast and its tail southwest. The greater part is owned today by individual islanders and the RSPB. A few properties are rented. There are several holiday homes. The resident population is currently in the region of 220.

Like the entire western seaboard of Scotland, Coll has a human history long and varied, particular to its location and topography. The earliest estimate of human habitation is between 7000–5000 BC. From the Stone Age through Neolithic, Celtic, Norse, Viking, Mediaeval and to more recent times the island has a legacy of stone circles, crannogs, brochs, duns, castles, crofts and farmhouses all with their own story to tell about the waves of incomers who have made a life and a living on its not-always-hospitable rock and heather, machair and sand dune terrain.

Ownership of land is a relatively modern concept in the Highlands and Islands of Scotland.

After the defeat and final withdrawal of the Norse from the Hebrides in 1263, Alexander III, King of Scotland, allowed Somerled, Lord of the Isles and progenitor of the powerful Clan Donald, to keep his title previously gifted by the Norse King Haakon. Other powerful clan chiefs subsequently became Lords of the Isles – the Macleans of Duart held a great part of Coll, Tiree, and lands on Islay and Jura. A settled period with mainland Scotland ensued but with an underlying distrust on the part of the Lords of the Isles who were not bound by the principle of primogeniture in selecting a chief.

Since 1124 the Anglo-Norman feudal system of land ownership had been adopted in Scotland. Clansmen, however, were freemen who had no part or understanding of that concept; the land was not 'owned' by them – or their chief.

But in 1493 James IV broke their united and threatening strength by dividing the predominant Clan Donald Lordship and created land holdings by Royal Charter. Those chiefs not co-operating had their lands forfeited.

Lawlessness in the Highlands and Islands ensued; it was clan against clan depending on who went with the King or fought for their chief and independence. When James VI succeeded to the English throne in 1603 the problem of the recurrent clan rebellions had to be dealt with; trade was being affected. A council held in Iona in 1609 resulted in all the chiefs agreeing to nine statutes cleverly crafted by the King to control individuality and disguise colonisation. Statute 1 demanded the acceptance of 'the discipline of the Reformed Kirk, maintaining the clergy and churches'. Statute 6: 'Every man having sixty cattle must send his eldest son to a Lowland school.' Statute 8: 'Bards who glorified war should be discouraged as idlers.'

The final destruction of the clan system was achieved 137 years later at Culloden in 1746.

After Culloden the Highlands and Islands were open to development and employment. The natives had been tamed; their leaders seduced for the first time into a money economy. First came the kelp industry. Then the herring and the black cattle. With relative prosperity the population rose. Clan chiefs no longer held communities together based on equality and territorial survival. They had become landowners, with all that the title entailed.

The chief was now called a Laird*. His land became an Estate, with fenced boundaries. His dependants had a new name, too: crofters. But their identity had not changed despite their chief's new title. They knew they and their forebears had worked land long held for the common good; they felt betrayed by their own kin. Mainland landowners and entrepreneurs also bought great swathes of land and donned the Laird's kilt. Their revolutionary industrial farming enterprises necessitated 'clearing' people from the fertile land.

These were bitter years of depression and destitution compounded by the potato blight of 1846 (which was not confined to Ireland) and a dramatic increase in population. But not all lairds were brutal: MacLean of Coll

---

* Scots variant of 'lard' – Middle English meaning lord, owner, master.

impoverished himself by providing boats and supplies for Collachs seeking new lives in Australia and New Zealand.

It was during this unsettled period, in 1856, that John Lorne Stewart, Factor to the Duke of Argyll, bought the major part of the island from the MacLeans and became the owner of Coll Estate and the first Stewart Laird of Coll. The land consisted of 18,000 acres and stretched from Crossapol to Cornaig. John Lorne Stewart was a renowned agriculturalist respected by some islanders for this reputation despite the inevitable 'movement' of many crofters from the fertile west end to the overcrowded and rock-strewn east end of the island. A residual bitterness nips some tongues to this day.

In the early 1880s, crofters in Tiree and Skye in particular violently rebelled against unjust rents and land laws. Johnstone of Totamore, a member of the Land League, supported the riots on Tiree but there is no record of violence on Coll. His monument stands up by Craig Darroch in the Village.

This unrest led to a Royal Commission enquiry and the creation of the Crofters' Holdings Act in 1886, which at last gave fair rent and security of tenure to the people of the Highlands and Islands.

But what, you may ask, has this, albeit brief, history to do with the last Laird of Coll?

It is the background to the story of the man who inherited Coll Estate in 1942 at the age of 18 and farmed its land for 50 years.

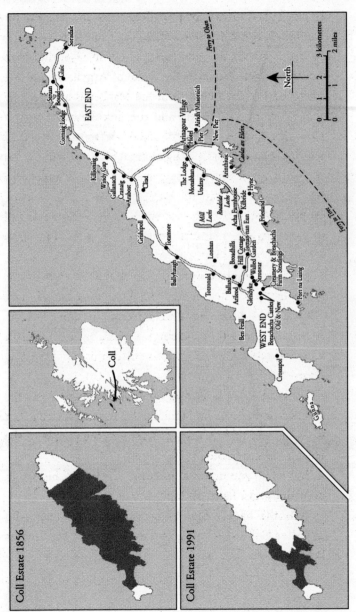

The Isle of Coll

Coll Estate 1856

Coll Estate 1991

EAST END

Sorisdale
Glaic
Struan
Bousd
Cornaig Lodge
Killiunaig
Windy Gap
Gallanach
Cornaig
Arnabost
Cliad
Grishipoll
Totamore
Ballyhaugh
Totronald
Arileod
Ben Feall
WEST END
Breachacha Castles
Old & New
Crossapol
Gunna
Port na Luing
Stronvar
Glendyke
Walled Garden
Creamery & Breachacha
Farm Steading
Uig
Hill Cottage
Broadhills
Ballard
Toman nan Eun
Acha Farmhouse
Kilbride
Friesland
Hyne
Arinthluic
Caolas an Eilein
New Pier
Pier
Ferry to Oban
Airidh Mhaoraich
Arinagour Village
Hotel
The Lodge
Monabhan
Undrag
Mill
Lochs
Roadside
Lochs

North

0   1   2   3 kilometres
0   1   2 miles

Ferry to Tiree

Coll

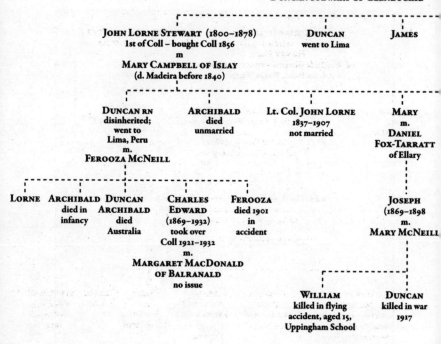

DUNCAN STEWART OF GLENBUCKIE

JOHN LORNE STEWART (1800–1878)
1st of Coll – bought Coll 1856
m
MARY CAMPBELL OF ISLAY
(d. Madeira before 1840)

DUNCAN
went to Lima

JAMES

DUNCAN RN
disinherited;
went to
Lima, Peru
m.
FEROOZA MCNEILL

ARCHIBALD
died
unmarried

Lt. Col. JOHN LORNE
1837–1907
not married

MARY
m.
**DANIEL
FOX-TARRATT**
of Ellary

LORNE

ARCHIBALD
died in
infancy

**DUNCAN
ARCHIBALD**
died
Australia

**CHARLES
EDWARD**
(1869–1932)
took over
Coll 1921–1932
m.
**MARGARET MACDONALD
OF BALRANALD**
no issue

FEROOZA
died 1901
in
accident

JOSEPH
(1869–1898
m.
MARY MCNEILL

WILLIAM
killed in flying
accident, aged 15,
Uppingham School

DUNCAN
killed in war
1917

SEVEN GENERATIONS OF THE STEWART LAIRDS OF COLL

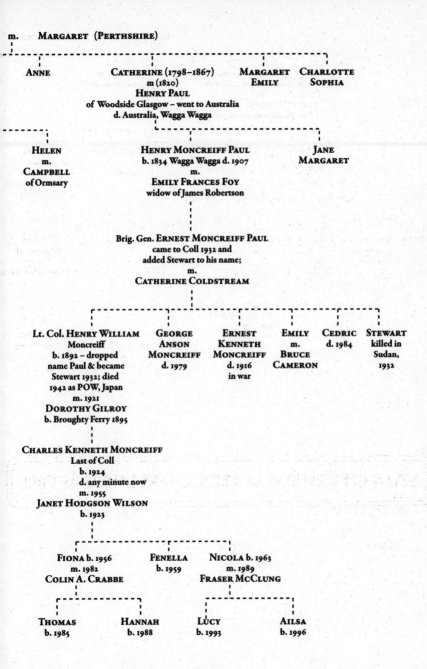

m. **MARGARET** (PERTHSHIRE)

ANNE **CATHERINE** (1798–1867) **MARGARET** **CHARLOTTE**
m (1820) **EMILY** **SOPHIA**
HENRY PAUL
of Woodside Glasgow – went to Australia
d. Australia, Wagga Wagga

HELEN **HENRY MONCREIFF PAUL** **JANE**
m. b. 1834 Wagga Wagga d. 1907 **MARGARET**
CAMPBELL m.
of Ormsary **EMILY FRANCES FOY**
widow of James Robertson

Brig. Gen. **ERNEST MONCREIFF PAUL**
came to Coll 1932 and
added Stewart to his name;
m.
CATHERINE COLDSTREAM

Lt. Col. **HENRY WILLIAM** **GEORGE** **ERNEST** **EMILY** **CEDRIC** **STEWART**
Moncreiff **ANSON** **KENNETH** m. d. 1984 killed in
b. 1892 – dropped **MONCREIFF** **MONCREIFF** **BRUCE** Sudan,
name Paul & became d. 1979 d. 1916 **CAMERON** 1932
Stewart 1932; died in war
1942 as POW, Japan
m. 1921
DOROTHY GILROY
b. Broughty Ferry 1895

CHARLES KENNETH MONCREIFF
Last of Coll
b. 1924
d. any minute now
m. 1955
JANET HODGSON WILSON
b. 1923

FIONA b. 1956 **FENELLA** **NICOLA** b. 1963
m. 1982 b. 1959 m. 1989
COLIN A. CRABBE **FRASER McCLUNG**

THOMAS **HANNAH** **LUCY** **AILSA**
b. 1985 b. 1988 b. 1993 b. 1996

The Stewart Family

Charles Kenneth Moncreiff Stewart was born in London in 1924. He was the only child of Dorothy Gilroy and Lt. Col. Henry William Moncreiff Paul. He had an older half-brother from the previous marriage of his mother who had been widowed in the First World War.

Henry, always known as Moncreiff, was a descendent of the Stewarts of Glenbuckie in Perthshire.

His great-great-grandmother was Catherine McNab Stewart. John Lorne Stewart, her brother and Moncreiff's great-great-uncle, became the first Stewart Laird of Coll in 1856. It was he who swept away the traditional ways and brought in new agricultural methods that put Coll on the map. Large dairy farms were established and the famous Coll cheeses and butter were exported to the Houses of Parliament and beyond.

His first son, Duncan, was disinherited. Lt. Col. John Lorne, the second son, never married. The grandsons of his sister Mary, married to Daniel Fox-Tarratt, were next in line but both were tragically killed – Duncan in the

First World War; William in a flying accident at school. Trustees ran the estate until their uncle, Charles Edward Stewart, took over in 1921. He died without issue in 1932 and was succeeded by his distant cousin, Moncreiff's father, Brigadier General Ernest Moncreiff Paul CBE RE Rtd., who, at the age of 68, added Stewart to his name by deed poll – as did his son. The Stewart line on Coll was secured.

Early Years

Did the little boy growing up in London know about the inheritance that awaited him on a remote Hebridean isle? He was told about it but didn't fully understand what it all meant.

Kenneth was a solitary child, possibly as a result of the calliper that he had to wear for many years to correct a foot defect at birth (his right foot had been turned backwards). His much older half-brother was away at school. He was close to his mother but in that distant style of the times. He remembers visiting museums and galleries in London with his father who, when not working at the War Office, enjoyed spending time with his son.

In 1934 Moncreiff was posted to Ismailia to join his regiment, which was stationed on the Suez Canal. He then became military attaché to the British Embassy in Bangkok. The Ambassador was not married so Kenneth's mother Dorothy acted as Embassy hostess. It was 1938 and interesting times. The King of Thailand was just about to be reinstated. They had the time of their lives.

One gets the impression of a somewhat lonely boy left behind in London, deeply attached to his Nanny. But the time of *his* life was just on the horizon.

∼ Holidays were spent on the Isle of Coll at the New Castle.* My grandfather, the Brigadier General, lived there except for the months between December to February when he would return to London. The castle was well maintained by an army of servants. Immediately after a storm there was always a flock of estate workers on the roof checking the slates.

Water was pumped from the well outside the front railing beyond the gravelled paths but it was just a wee lean-to shed to the left of the castle entrance that was the toilet. A hydraulic ram in the stackyard provided more water from the burn essential for the creamery. The steadings were a hive of activity with the Estate lorry collecting and delivering churns of milk from the tenant farms. My grandfather, being an engineer, had hopes of taking water from the Mill Lochs to make electricity. But nothing came of it. The supply was too doubtful in summer. Though the fish stocked by my grandfather were plentiful.

There was an old bridge that could take a cart over to the walled garden at the end of the Castle Park where flower and vegetable beds had hedges all round. A huge greenhouse leaned against one wall. Fruit trees and bushes everywhere.

I was nine years old the first time I went to Coll with my father, mother and Nanny. It was 1933. We drove up from London, staying with friends on the way. At Oban my mother went to great lengths to shorten the

---

* Always called the New Castle, it was built by the Macleans in 1750 close by the ruins of their ancestral home, the Old Castle.

sea journey for she was terrified of boats and the sea. We crossed to Tobermory in the *Loch Fyne* which was very modern with electric motors charged up by diesel generators. It had two funnels but one was a dummy. For a small boy this was all very exciting.

We stayed overnight in the Western Isles Hotel in Tobermory on Mull, although I was put to bed far too early, I thought. Next day the *Lochmor* pounded us over to Coll. My mother did not die. True to form the old General came alongside in the ferryboat and we were whisked to the New Castle in the Humber, one of only three cars on the island at that time.

I was terrified of my Grandfather. He was very severe and churchy and grumpy.

Nanny and I were closeted in the housekeeper's room, except for when we were dragged into the dining room for morning prayers before breakfast. All the staff and servants were in attendance and everyone had to kneel on the floor whilst my grandfather read from the bible and prayed and prayed. On a Sunday he would get a trailer hitched to the back of the car to give islanders at the West End a lift to church in the Village. He would charge sixpence.

He was very mean. Once he gave me a half-crown. My other grandfather gave £1 every Christmas. My great-aunts gave me ten shillings.

Whenever I saw him I ran for my life. He would shout out over the Castle Park, 'Don't dare run away from me, boy! Come here at once!' I wouldn't turn back and had to pay sore for my rudeness later on.

I fled from the castle whenever I could. I loved going to the neighbouring farms where I was always welcomed. My escapes to Arileod, Lonban and Ballard were where my love of farming started, I'm sure. Oh! and the piggery at Breachacha where I carried the whey in pails from the cheese making to the young pigs in the pens. Nanny was not pleased at that. ∾

There was a romance between Nanny and Mr Patmore. Gilbert Patmore was Moncreiff's batman who had also come to the island for the first time. He had travelled north by train for the historic visit. A trained mechanic, Patmore, as he was always called, was invaluable. The Humber and the Wolseley were well looked after. He was soon to become the General's chauffeur and factotum.

The next year, 1933, saw the couple married in London. They moved with Kenneth and his mother to live on Coll. The Patmores settled at Acha farmhouse where Patmore created the first windmill to generate electricity on the island.

Kenneth's mother rented Acha schoolhouse from the Estate. His father's commitments with the War Office kept him in London save for holidays with the family.

∾ The Acha teacher stayed in the Hotel. She was Miss Mitchell, daughter of the Tobermory pier master.

When I came to Acha on holiday sometimes the school was still open and I played with Wee Morag and Flora (teacher to be) and barefoot Nina. Always girls! But then I do remember playing *Take the Bulls to the Boat* with the boys. We'd wrap ropes round someone's head and legs and pull the unfortunate 'bull' the length of the field. ∾

After a series of small schools including Elmhurst and St Mary's, Colchester, Kenneth went to Durnford Prep School near Swanage in Dorset and finally on to Wellington.

Acha and the island were always waiting to be enjoyed during the holidays without the rigours of staying at the New Castle.

∾ Acha had to have some alterations. A tiny room was created upstairs for our two maids Katie and Lexie from Arinthluic. The two of them slept in the same bed. Probably did the same at home. Don't think they ever took their clothes off. I see it differently now looking back but at that time as long as they stayed out of the way and got on with their work all was well. They survived with us for a couple of years.

Most families lived in very cramped conditions. Two families lived in Hill Cottage in just two rooms. The island was hoaching with people. Especially up the East End. ∾

That first year of residency was carefully noted by the islanders, east and west. Although the General was still all-powerful and dominant his son and grandson were welcomed by all with an interest in the future. No more so than the tenants at Totronald.

∾ One morning my mother, father and myself were at breakfast in Acha when a knock came at the door. It was one of the younger Totronalds. 'My mother wants you to come for a meal tonight,' she said.

Dumbfounded, my father managed to convey thanks and acceptance. My mother was quite taken aback. Nothing had happened like this before.

My parents did not know what to expect. But we all got dressed up and arrived at Totronald at the appointed time to be taken 'down to the room' for a couple of drinks and then told to go 'up to the kitchen'. You always went 'down' to the best room and 'up' to the kitchen.

The table was groaning with enormous plates of meat. Then bowls of pudding and plates of scones and cakes were handed round by 'Mother Dear'. We were stuffed. All the MacLeans talking the while and enjoying themselves. But that was not the end of it. It was down to the room again for more drinks and talk. And then we escaped.

There was something special about the people on Coll, I think. They did not stand on ceremony.

Yet Father Totronald became very staid on the Sabbath. Nobody was allowed to work except for milking and feeding the cows. That's why the grip there was made much wider than the usual. Monday morning it took 30 to 40 barrows to muck out the byre.

I was told Billy Connolly's granny – or great-granny, was it? – came from Totronald. ∼

* * *

Friesland farm, near to Acha, became a favourite haunt of the young boy who would disappear there for hours on end.

∼ The Kennedys treated me like family. Old Andrew had been the Estate joiner before going to Friesland. He was full of rheumatism. His second wife, Mary Ann, was a great baker and very straight talking. Once I seriously needed the toilet. She handed me a bucket and a sheet of *The Bulletin* newspaper and told me to go into the stable. It was like that back then. That was the kind of life one led. We had two Elsans [*chemical toilet*] at Acha, which was very superior.

My grandfather provided an Elsan for a lot of households but not everyone appreciated the latest in sanitation. He was called the Laird of the Loos. 'I've been going up the burn all my life and I'll keep on doing that,' said Mhor Vhor from Uig. The General remonstrated with her but it was no use. She had already set a hen on eggs in it. 'It's better than a box,' she said.

Don't know what they used the Elsan for at Friesland.

Later on when I was farming the Estate I got called the Laird of the Loos, too. I gradually installed water sanitation in all the farmhouses.

Neilly, Angus, young Andrew and Flora at Friesland were great fun but best of all was riding the horse, Polly. She was a quiet, easy horse.

Summer visitors often stayed at Friesland. They always took preference as far as Mother Friesland was concerned. Even at hay time, should she have run out of, say, ham or bread, Neilly would be dispatched immediately to the Village.

At night when the tide was in, Friesland was a wonderful, beautiful place. But smelly when the tide was out. Still one of my favourite places – that and Port na Luing. ∽

Aged 13 Kenneth became the proud owner of his first cow, bought by his mother for £16. Alan and Hughie Lonban had handpicked the animal for her gentle nature. She was called Brownie and came with a calf. In time Kenneth would have 300 cows grazing the dunes of Feall.

Holidays were not spent completely in fields and farmyards. Summertime brought an influx of visitors. Some arrived in large yachts and anchored in Breachacha Bay. Beach parties on fine days were very much part of the social scene.

A young girl called Janet Hodgson-Wilson and her sister Marjorie were regular holidaymakers, coming with their mother, Phillis Hinkson, to visit her brother Billy

Colyer-Fergusson. Uncle Billy had met the General on one of those yachting trips to Coll from Mull and had stayed, attracted by the shooting and fishing on the Estate. The two were great friends; Billy was a very good shot and fisherman and a keen naturalist.

Thanks to the General and his predecessors and their gamekeepers the island had an abundance of game and fish for sport.

Railings were fixed to the sheer sea cliff at Ben Feall for the gentry to gun down the wild ducks and pigeons returning to roost and the ladies safely to watch the sun set. Peregrines made feast of the thousands of pigeons, too, and raised chicks each year on the high clefts in the rock.

Snipe, curlew, grouse, partridge, woodcock, golden plover were there for the having, to say nothing of geese, duck, rabbit and hare. A day's bag for two guns was thirty to forty head of feathered game.

The moors were regularly burned to encourage new heather growth for the grouse. The General was very keen on that. Controlled alternative strips were burned with military precision annually. The burned area was left for a couple of years for the heather to grow and the grouse to flourish.

The New Castle game books are almost shocking to read today.

Kenneth grew up with this backdrop of privileged pleasures, little knowing he would one day use the rusted and collapsing railings to retrieve sheep fallen into gullies in the bare rock of Ben Feall, not a peregrine in sight and the New Castle behind him, silent and deserted.

As a boy he liked nothing better than helping out on the farms, learning the old methods and hearing the old stories but no doubt also enjoying the parallel world of beach parties and picnics.

⌐ Helping in the hayfield one day, raking the hay into rucks, I saw everyone running about looking at the ground. There were little balls in the grass. Bumble bee nests. Callum Limetree was guddling them up in handfuls and squeezing them. He gave me one. 'Try that. It's good,' he said. It was full of honey.

The only fertilisers were dung and seaweed. All horse drawn. Bogging on Breachacha beach was a seasonal hazard. Sutherland, the smith at Caolis an Eilean, turned rough ground into a twice-cut pasture on account of the quantity of seaweed he layered on.

There was a lot of rivalry between the farmers and the crofters to be the first finished at harvesting. Especially between Gallanach and Cliad. But Lachie Ballard could put up a stook in an evening single-handed.

Everyone was their own vet in those days. I saw some horrific sights. Cows with difficult births, the calf's legs hanging out and the owner dismembering the half-born, but thankfully dead, calf to save the cow. Usually the cow died too. It's a huge injection of penicillin nowadays before you do anything. And it's a blood test from the tail today. Then it was a tightened loop round the neck of the cow to bring up the vein.

There was a Ministry vet, very religious, from Skye who told anyone who swore to get out of the byre. There was a lot of swearing when the men were working with cattle.

Once the vet came over from Tiree but that was only to inspect a hired stallion that had died for insurance purposes. Most of the time everyone just got on with it.

Lachie Hector at Arileod was good at everything, the old men said. An imposing figure in the West End, he could save your cow and castrate your calf, no bother.

Barter was the currency. The smith would shoe horses for a day's ploughing. Fish would be swapped for a cockerel or a hen. In those days when someone was needing help with the hay or the peats or the clipping you did your bit and then they helped you.

And always the farmers would go on about Callum Limetree's Highlanders at his Bousd croft at the East End. 'He has 16 and there is 3 ft between their horns . . .'

Callum showed me how to make little coils of hay before making rucks. He was the same man who, when reaching the steep Windy Gap halfway home with his horse and cart, would take one of the sacks onto his shoulder. 'Good for the horse,' he would say. ∼

Kenneth's memory of these times is coloured so much by the characters that he got to know and understand from childhood and into adulthood. They belonged to an era that passed within Kenneth's lifetime. Gaelic-speaking for the most part, their spoken English was a delight to the ear of someone whose formal southern education could have isolated him.

∼ I tried to learn Gaelic, picking it up from the men in the first place and then going for lessons from the Teacher, a local Gaelic speaker, but she kept correcting the Gaelic I had learned from the men. Back at the fank or the field the men were having none of her corrections. I gave up in the end though I could often get the gist of what was going on. ∼

He loved the twists and turns of local events and politics recounted with that particular type of insightful humour that is found in small island communities, where individuals and groups are ever watchful for the failings and *faux pas* of others. He no doubt enjoyed hearing tales about the General as well.

~ Sturgeon was the island shopkeeper and postmaster. He rented the shop in the Village from the Estate.

Sturgeon had a falling out with Charles Edward Stewart on account of wanting the post office only. The impasse was resolved – by Sturgeon's way of it – in a most ingenious way. He built a shed on stilts that stood over the tideline nearby. Up went the telegraph pole and Sturgeon had won. He ran his business on Crown property until my grandfather gave in and the post office was finally moved to the Sturgeon home at Tigh na Mara, which is what Sturgeon wanted in the first place.

Another enterprise did not end so happily. Sturgeon decided to try beekeeping and was pleased when the bees went over to the other side of the loch to Airidh Mhaoraich where the heather was sweet. They disappeared. 'Drooned in the water on the way back,' said a local.

Much later on there was a shopkeeper called William Sproat who came from Mull. His shop, originally a tin byre from Alexsandach's croft, was on the breest of the slope opposite Limetree on the village street. Not quite into the water but near enough.

Telephoning his weekly order to the merchants in Glasgow he was quite taken aback by the response of an answering machine. 'Mar Cheer!' he responded before giving his lengthy order. ('Mar cheer' is phonetic for 'mo dia', meaning 'my God'.) The order came in due course with a note attached saying *'Enclosed tub of margarine as requested'*. ~

The twins, Hector and Archie at Sorasdale, were always a source of remembered delight to Kenneth despite the trepidations of going to the foreign territory of the East End to visit them.

~ Going to the East End of the island, which was never owned by the Stewarts, was like going into deepest Africa. It was so far away. A day's journey if you didn't have a car. I went for the first time with my mother in 1935. She was collecting for the Silver Jubilee George V Playing Fields for Children Fund. Trailing behind her I wondered how on earth the people survived. Rocks everywhere and the fields so small. Unbelievably, everyone gave a shilling or a sixpence.

Umpteen people living in those tiny houses; some, if they were lucky, existing on half an acre. There was a red-haired woman called Augusta (we all called her Gusta) who lived in a minute cottage – a stone hut, really – beyond Struan. She could carry a bag of flour under each arm from the village when she was young.

The folk were all very poor and TB was rife. There was TB screening after the Second World War but many islanders wouldn't go. So many family members had died. They did not want to know. Whenever a house came up in the village the East Enders were the first to apply.

First time I went to a dance in the village I couldn't believe the number of young lads from the East End. Where had they all come from? Who was related to who? 'Bred like rabbits,' my mother would say. It was several years before I knew everybody. I only got to know Johnny Glaic when he got his toes shot off whilst gillie for the shooting clients. He was taken to the West End for the air ambulance. Some East Enders had never been to the Village.

I wouldn't go to Sorisdale in the dark. A funny feeling. Hidden territory. But everyone was so polite and friendly to speak to. The Twins were so genuine. No feeling of 'Oh! Here comes a Sassanach, an incomer.'

Their thatched crofthouse was right on the edge of the bay with a view out to Mull. Always with a weather eye to sea they would note the boats coming and going. Passengers on a cruise ship that regularly passed would wave to the two old botachs. One day a letter came addressed 'To the Two Old Grey-haired Men at Sorisdale'. Inside, with best wishes, it said: 'We do enjoy passing and seeing you wave.'

'Och!' said Hector. 'They must have seen my hair when I took my hat off to wave.'

Hector took the cattle and Archie, the sheep, to market in Oban. Their elder brother Neil did the housekeeping. Always called 'the boy', he was a youngster of 54. The trio were joined by Johnny MacInnes from Glaic when his parents died. It was a bachelor's domain.

The Twins had their own chair each side of the fire. When the television came to Coll they had grand reception direct from Skye. But one would be sitting face on, the other craning his neck back like a bird to see the screen. Then Johnny would come in, always at a critical time, and change programmes.

It is not that I am laughing at the East Enders. It was just that they had attitudes and mannerisms unchanged for hundreds of years. Maybe moulded by memories of hardship and rejection at the time of the clearances from the West End.

I was only once made to feel uncomfortable about being a Stewart by an old islander, Hector McDougall, who had to make a point of telling me that my family had 'ruined the island by clearing everyone off from the West End to the East End'. I was ten years old when he told me that.

I was always interested in the islanders whether employed by the estate or not. As an adult I would arrange with MacBrayne's for the boat to take the East End crofters' stock to market. There were three boats that came in October to pick up the Coll stock, one in May for cattle and one in August for lambs.

For all the years I was on Coll I never had any troubles with the crofters. Neilly John would ask 'Can I go up to Monabhan, meaning the fair moss, to cut some thatch for my stack?' I'd reply, 'Yes, sure, Neilly John, as long as you leave me some.' And he would. ∼

The War and the New Laird

On leaving Wellington Kenneth went to Cambridge to study for a Degree in Agriculture. The Second World War was well under way. All travellers had to have permits with photos signed by the Army. On journeys home Kenneth sometimes had difficulty in convincing the officious Army Captain in Oban that he was the General's grandson.

Moncreiff was on active service in the Far East, Dorothy staying at Acha. On his visits back to the island Kenneth experienced Coll's war.

⁓ There was regular submarine activity. Angus at Arinthluic came upon a man leaning on a rock by the shore. Thinking him asleep he went up to him to wake him. The German submariner was dead. They buried him in Killionaig. After the War the remains were returned to Germany. Other bodies were washed up on different parts of the island. A temporary mortuary was set up at the back of the Lodge. One coffin was for the pilot of a British Hurricane reconnaissance plane that came down at Hyne.

I remember seeing the old steamship the *Hebrides*,

full of airmen going to Tiree. They were shoved down the hold like cattle and there was a ruddy machine gun on the poop at the stern in case of U-boats.

My grandfather organised the Home Guard, of course. Everyone joined. Even Neilly John. Guard huts were built at Toman nan Eun and Arnabost for a rota of two men each night. A sergeant major came from the Edinburgh barracks to drill the volunteers. In the finish up he told them they all 'looked like a lot of babies' nappies'. Old George from Lonban was so taken aback he got on his bike and went home. Neilly John's mother, Peggy, made him go to the hotel and resign.

There was a lot of wreck washed up. My grandfather thought it was all his. But most folk hid anything useful that they found. There was a report of a mine come up on Sloc Mhor gully at the back of Totronald. Alan Lonban going for gravel had seen it. A big expedition was got together by my grandfather. He said he would deal with it. 'General Stewart, Sir,' said Alan, 'I found the mine and I have reported it to Mr Bremner, the Receiver of Wreck. You have no right to come here and expect to have anything to do with it.'

A hell of a row ensued. I knew Alan had a temper but nothing like this. I got a fearful fright. But no more than my grandfather who wasn't accustomed to being talked to like this by what he would call a peasant.

In the finish up nobody did anything about it. Eventually three men came from the mainland and blew it up. The sheep ran for miles.

There were a lot of mines floating in the sea. A low-flying plane spotter saw one going in to Sorisdale bay. The Twins, Hector and Archie, were working at corn and looked up to see the pilot throwing something out of the plane. They thought it was a bomb. Hector and Archie dived under the stooks. Nothing happened.

Eventually they crawled out and found a bottle on the

shore with a message in it. At the Smiddy in the Village the next Saturday, when they were getting supplies, they regaled the locals with the tale. The message said, they claimed, MINE APPROACHING BAY. EXCAVATE HOUSE IMMEDIATELY. 'What did you do?' they were asked. Did nothing, they replied, but kept hidden. 'For what would we do with the horses?' But the message had in fact said: MINE APPROACHING BAY. EVACUATE HOUSE IMMEDIATELY. ∼

After three years at Cambridge, Kenneth was called up for an army medical. The doctor noticed the deformed foot. 'You have had polio,' he categorically stated. In denying this Kenneth was called a liar and dismissed as unfit.

A tutor suggested a job with the college's farm team in Yorkshire to dig up soil samples. Kenneth had a better idea. He contacted his mother on Coll and got her to write to the War Agricultural Executive Committee in Oban explaining about the Estate having no factor or manager and that her son should get dispensation to go back home to run the farm and Estate. It worked. Kenneth was where he wanted to be and the serious business of learning from scratch in his chosen career had begun.

∼ I read many books and got advice from the college but a lot of my practical apprenticeship was at Lonban with Alan and Hughie. Alan's temper could be sudden and I had to watch my step. I learned how to tie the two horses to the plough and drive them with the reaper and the rake. I had to forget everything I had learned at Cambridge. Farming methods in East Anglia were irrelevant.

Ballard and Arileod showed interest in my willingness to learn, too. The tenant farmers were supportive. Gave me encouragement. 'Let's see how the young lad can do,' kind of thing. My grandfather never went near the farms.

I was shown by Donald Walker how to sow corn. He took me to Breachacha beach and filled the sowing sheet with sand. It took a while to coordinate my strides with the alternate swinging of my arms and throwing the sand in an arc. But I did it.

When the guy that did the sowing left I got the job and I've used that method ever since. I could do ten acres in two or three hours and loved the rhythm and movement. At the start of the day sacks of corn would be placed in a row at the top and the bottom of the field. Someone would be there to fill up the sowing sheet as you were moving so as not to break the rhythm. Couldn't stand the fiddliness of a corn seeder, pushing that handle back and forth.

I don't suppose you could buy a sowing sheet these days. ∽

* * *

It was 1942. Kenneth and the men were cutting corn in the field behind Glendyke. The old General had died six months previously. Kenneth's father was fighting in the Far East and unaware of his inheritance. For Kenneth there was a sense of relief now that his grandfather was no longer dominating his life – and that of his father. Moncreiff and the General did not get on with each other. Kenneth looked forward to his father coming back and the two of them running the Estate together.

It was a perfect day. The weather would hold for the

week, the men said. The stacks would get up high and dry no bother. Mid-morning Kenneth could see Patmore walking over the stubble towards him.

He brought shocking news. Henry William Moncreiff Stewart OBE, MC and *Chevalier de la Légion d'honneur*, was dead. He had died of dysentery in a prisoner of war camp in Japan where he had been imprisoned for several months. Moncreiff, with many others, had been captured in Hong Kong after their troopship had been torpedoed.

'You are now the Laird of Coll,' said Patmore.

～ I could only think of my mother – twice widowed by war. And then I felt so bereft and lost and absolutely terrified of what was ahead of me. If I had been a confident and enterprising man I would have hopped on a plane to sort out our affairs. But money was tight.

We travelled the long journey to Edinburgh to meet up with the lawyers. That's when I learned the unpalatable facts. The Estate was bankrupt. No factor, no this, no that. The farm at Acha which I had started to develop was in dire financial straits. Add to that double death duties. The Estate was entailed. There was no way out of it. That bloody island, I thought.

My half-brother was with the army in France so it was just my mother and myself rattling about in the Roxburghe Hotel in Edinburgh. She was so distressed. I had to keep my feelings to myself. There was nothing for it but to get back to Coll and get on with it.

In due course we were sent a little photo of the war grave. My father was given a posthumous DSO. ～

Back on Coll the War Effort dictated a relentless routine. Kenneth and his mother lived in Acha by themselves. Kenneth got up at 6 a.m. to hand-milk the cows for Acha and the farm workers' families before the day's work began. Dorothy tackled the bookkeeping. She took to chain-smoking and smoking a pipe when cigarettes ran out. Kenneth had no one to confide in and wanted to spare his mother his concerns.

~ I knew I had to grow up. The first hurdle was to get the confidence to go with the stock when they went to the sales in Oban. That was horrific to begin with. Then I got into the way of it, bidding with the rest of them. I began to realise I had an eye for a good beast. Little did I know I would become a Director of Corson's Mart one day and later Vice Chairman from 1968 to '88 when the Mart was amalgamated with United Auctions in Perth and Stirling.

I killed and butchered four sheep a week during the war to distribute as meat ration to the islanders. I had to fix lids halfway down the ropes in the byre to stop rats getting to the carcasses. Whoever got gigot one week got neck the next. I was very fair about that.

A lot of men had to stay on the island to maintain the cheese and butter industry and didn't get called up. The Milk Marketing Board took over the creamery and cheese making at the Estate farm at Breachacha. That was when the tenant farmers stopped making cheese themselves and just delivered milk to the creamery. The Government was not giving subsidies for dairying but for beef production. The Ayrshire dairy cows started to be sold off. They hardly got a penny. ~

The war on Coll had its compensations. Dorothy's craving for cigarettes was well sated when the convoy ship *Nevada* went on the Struan rocks at the East End on a fog-bound flat calm summer's day in 1942.

Coll has had its fair share of wrecks along the coastline but this one was in the league of a *Whisky Galore* spectacular. The *Nevada* had 7,000 tons of NAAFI cargo on board heading for West Africa. Jeeps, motor parts, tools, bales of Manchester cotton, surgical supplies and much more. Crates of cigarettes and whisky. It also transpired that she had hundreds of pounds worth of African currency in boxes in the hold.

The *Nevada*'s fog horn alerted those at the East End and by the time she had gone aground many islanders had crowded onto the rocks that held her fast. With the aid of a bosun's chair the African crew were hauled the short distance to safety where they all proceeded to kneel on the rocks and pray to Allah.

The French Captain and the only English-speaking crew member, the wireless operator, stayed on board to defend the ship. They had to. Locals were already boarding. It was wartime after all. The wireless operator was reduced to waving his revolver and telling the islanders to put back items heading for the shore.

Judging by the stories still recounted with envy and awe it would appear that the guarding of the *Nevada* was but a token affair. In the interval between the grounding and the arrival of the Customs officers great quantities of booty found their way to hidden places all over the island.

Night time was raid time. When the tide came in the hold filled with water and crates of cigarettes floated to the surface. The cigarettes were in round sealed tins of fifty. Woodbines were thrown back into the sea; Players No. 3 and Capstan being much superior. The emptied Woodbine tins were convenient for quaffing the whisky in comradely ceilidhs on the shore between forays into the hold. Carts took crate loads of bottles to byres, up into lofts and underneath beds.

~~ I got thousands of cigarettes for my mother. The irony was that, after months of there being no cigarettes on the island and Sturgeon at the shop complaining to the Government, suddenly he was not pleased when the very weekend of the grounding of the *Nevada* the authorities decided to increase his quota. Nobody bought cigarettes from the shop for two years.

Some say there is still whisky buried in the sand dunes. People forgot where they had buried the bottles. The more alcoholic members of the community mixed the surgical spirit with water and added brown sugar to colour it. One man nearly killed himself. There were monumental hangovers.

Islanders stole from islanders. The Twins, Hector and Archie at Sorisdale, the gentlest of old souls, set off in their boat in the dark of night to see what they could get from the wreck. A substantial haul was rowed back and the boat pulled up on a hidden shore a bit away from their croft, the two of them planning to come at daybreak to load the cart. Hearing voices they ran for home, thinking it could be an official party.

Next morning the boat was empty, the Twins incensed. At the following weekly Saturday visit to the Village they were heard to say, 'If we had known we were in the right we would have called the Bobby!'

All hell broke loose when the Customs men did come. I ran up the back of Acha and stuffed tins of cigarettes down the rabbit holes. For they had authority to inspect houses. Many people used rabbit holes that way. The rabbit trappers then couldn't get on with their work, which was big business during the war. The rabbits were jammed safe behind the tins.

Another part of the cargo was hundreds of pairs of brown patent-leather shoes. For years everyone had shiny new shoes at the dances and navy blue tunic tops.

Bales of cotton were dried on washing lines and colourful curtains, cushions and bedspreads appeared. Neilly John's mother, Peggy, had already speedily redecorated her home when the Customs man came through the door. 'Any material?' he asked. 'Not as much as would cover your birdy,' she replied, staring him in the eye and she half blind herself.

It was 20 years after the salvage that £19,749 in shilling notes belonging to the West African Currency Board showed up for exchange. Nobody will know exactly what happened. Were Collachs involved? They say of the ten boxes that were in the hold two and a half were empty. They say an elder of the church, amongst others, took his share. But people can be so two-faced, you know.

There was a court case in Edinburgh. Jimmy Bousd was a witness, his croft being near the wreck. He wore a trilby hat. ⌁

Post-war Challenges

~

The war ended but post-war agricultural depression was particularly hard in remote locations like Coll which had limited communications and employment opportunities. Islanders looked to the mainland for another way of life. Dairying had come to an end, the cheese-making equipment going finally to Islay in 1952. The population was decreasing. When Kenneth first went to Coll the population was 300. It slowly dwindled to an all-time low of 129 by late 1950.

Kenneth was determined to keep going. His half-brother, Alastair Carré, came to live at the Lodge in the village, acting as factor for the Estate and leaving Kenneth to get on with the farm, which was his preferred occupation.

~ During the war it was obligatory to plough up extra ground. The fields by the burn at Ballard had not been cropped for a long time. The ground was too wet. But after fifty years ley, what a crop they got.

And I drained everywhere, too. There were masses of

old tile drains dug up and replaced. If only the land had been maintained over the years. So quickly it can revert. I opened up the big field at Port na Luing. There was a loch with a crannog there where an eighteenth-century sword had been found long before my time. I unblocked all the drains. No archaeological embargos in those days. Blasted the rock at the end of the ditch that was a death trap for animals. I made a garden out of that field with mixed crops.

We still have the sword. It was used by Charles Stewart of Ardshiel in a duel with Rob Roy McGregor at Balquhidder Inn. They say it must stay in the family or else we shall have bad luck.

The Acha field was pure peat up towards the loch. Incidentally that is where the stone came from for the war memorial in the Village. That field and all the way to Kilbride was ploughed and turned into arable. Kilbride steading was built – before my time – with stones from the ancient graveyard there. A stone fell off the roof and killed a man. Taking the gravestones was blamed.

The other obsession I had was fencing. I fenced and fenced.

It was tempting to plough the Castle Park, as it used to be called, but I'd heard about the disaster in my great grandfather's time. They had ploughed it up and seeded it with corn the first year. It became a field of blown sand. Same with the fields to Port na Luing. You could see all the way to Crossapol from the Castle, the ground bare with windblown sand and stones. Then they tried turnips and that didn't work. It took years for the sand to be stabilised by marram grass in the dunes and grass successfully reseeded in the Castle Park.

Weather wise, my farming memories are sometimes as grey as the winter weather was. I remember endless gales, much worse than now, cattle leaning against walls for shelter. Some people actually suffered from 'wind madness' as it was called. It was always wet as far as I was concerned.

The fields would be littered with dead lambs in the spring. The sheep had two and three lambs usually. Before lambing I'd dig a huge hole – six to eight feet deep. If it was a bad lambing I'd dig another. Dead sheep and lambs went to the bents (dunes). Horses and cattle went to the back of Stronvar.

Easter time was fraught with distressed holiday people coming to the house just as I'd be getting my boots off for the day and reporting the whereabouts of a dead lamb or sheep. There were several corpses in front of Totronald once and I was reported to the police. Boots, as we called the policeman, came over and we had a hell of a row. 'I'm not interested in the dead,' I yelled. 'I'm only interested in the living!'

But if I think again there were sunny days. I remember getting the peats in and the dust rising in the road in front of the carts. I think the weather was drier in the '30s and '40s.

There was a severe drought in 1968. It went on for weeks. All the burns dry. The Totronald cows were walked over the hill to the Mill Lochs via Totamore. Ballard drove theirs to the Roadside Lochs. People in the West End collected water from there and the women washed clothes and themselves during the day in the lochs. The men washed at night. ∼

Fraser Darling, the eminent naturalist and agriculturalist, was commissioned in 1942 by the Scottish Secretary of State to develop an advisory programme for the future of the Highlands and Islands. He travelled extensively throughout the area observing and assessing and came to Coll a few years later after a sojourn camping on Lunga, one of the Treshnish Isles. The last residents on Lunga had left in 1856 so Fraser Darling was presumably studying wildlife as opposed to humans.

With him came C.M. Grieve (Hugh MacDiarmid) and a group of other 'experts' each with ideas for reviving the economy of Coll and Tiree. Darling was not in favour of sheep and championed the return of dairy farming. In his subsequent publication, *West Highland Survey*, published in 1955, he stated that 350 to 400 people could be supported by this industry whereas the keeping of store cattle would provide too small a population for a viable society.

But it was all too late. There was no government enthusiasm for revitalising the dairy industry on Coll. It was difficult enough attracting farm workers to a depopulating island that had no electricity or pier.

Grieve gave examples of bracken eradication on Mull and the guidance of the MacAulay Soil Institute in Aberdeen as the way forward. Darling also proposed that Crossapol, deserted at the time, be used for the site of an Agricultural College for both Tiree and Coll with a bridge connection between both islands. The possibility of a new deep-water pier for Coll with a daily boat service to and from Tiree was discussed if the bridge was not viable.

It was a convivial night in the village hall with drams flowing.

Nobody talked about electricity.

'Aye, grand ideas,' said a local afterwards, 'but once they leave the island we'll hear no more.'

Slowly but surely the island population further declined. *Old People's Island* was the title of environmentalist John Barr's article in 1963 for *New Society*, then the sister publication to the *New Statesman*. Sadly, his outsider's

Catherine McNab Stewart, married Henry Paul, 1820.

The Paul family, 1910. Left to right: Anson, Millie, Kenneth, Ernest Moncreiff Paul, Cedric, Henry, Catherine (Kate), Stewart.

Above. Young Kenneth Stewart with family at Breachachar New Castle, 1934. Left to right: Cedric (uncle), Henry Moncrieff (father), Peter Carré (half brother), Dorothy (mother), Kenneth Stewart, Ernest Moncrieff (grandfather).

Left. Brigadier General Ernest Moncreiff Paul. Breachachar Castle. The Stewart name was adopted in 1932.

The Castle car with trailer returning from church, 1934.

The Brigadier General's Annual Boys' Brigade summer camp at Crossapol beach.

The wedding of Lieutenant Colonel Henry Moncreiff Paul and Dorothy Gilroy, 1921.

Kenneth aged three.

Left. Kenneth dancing a Highland fling at Colchester.

Above. Feeding the pigs at the Castle farm at Breachacha

Beolved Polly at Freisland

On the *Loch Earn* with Patmore and Nanny.

Above. Acha School House, Kenneth's first and last home on Coll, 1934.

Above right. Schoolboy Kenneth at Durnford, Dorset.

Right. Engagement to Janet, 1955, Baron's Court Road, London

Below. Wedding of Charles Kenneth Moncreiff Stewart to Janet Hodgson-Wilson at St Michael's, Chester Street, London, 1955.

Above left. Daughters Fiona, Nicola and Fenella, 1964.

Above right. Working cattle on Gunna.

Left. The ferry boat with Davy Fotheringham at the tiller.

Below. MV *Claymore* coming alongside the new pier for the first time, 1967.

Above left. Plaque of thanks from the people of Coll to Captain Jimmy Campbell, May 1989.

Above right. The arable farmer.

Right. Kenneth and daughter Nicola with some of the rare-breed sheep.

Below right. Judging at the Tiree Show.

Bottom. The New Castle and Breachacha steadings.

Left. Setting off for Luing Cattle Sales, 1974.

Below left. Kenneth with the Highlanders, after his stroke, 1989

Bottom. Stock leaving Coll at the time of the sale of the estate, 1991.

Above. Kenneth Stewart leaving Coll. John McKechnie, stock man, is on the right.

Right. Kenneth and Janet retired in the Borders, 1992.

view of an ageing and diminishing community, spinsters and bachelors forming a disproportionate part of the community, was not received kindly by the islanders. But there were truths that had to be accepted. The population *was* diminishing.

Suffice it to say, John Barr and his wife, Pat, came to own Hyne soon afterwards. They were regular half-yearly residents and part of the first flights of Summer Swallows whose descendents still come and boost the island economy today.

* * *

It wasn't until 1967 that the deep-water pier was completed, having been started in 1964. Electricity didn't arrive until 1979. The daily boat to and from Tiree never materialised. Neither did the bridge.

〜 The Agricultural College had already tried to get the farmers to diversify by growing beet. Against their instinct they co-operated. The beet did grow. Cartloads were taken to the pier to await collection by a puffer. It never came. The piles of beet started to rot. John Ballyhaugh sent an angry telegram to the college. SEND SHIP IMMEDIATELY. BEET FLOURISHING. He meant to say PERISHING. It made no difference. The boat still didn't come.

I had my own disasters. Enthusiastic still with ideas from college days I grew mangolds and *sainfoin* for winter feed. In Cambridge they got two crops a year. I tried – and with linseed – but they didn't ripen. I should have known to forget all I'd learned about farming in Cambridge when I set foot on Coll. Heavens, we were still using horses.

The authorities were forever sending bits of paper. When fowl pest was rampant on the mainland in '49 we had to record the number of birds on the island. Then slaughter them all. They were not infected. But we had to comply with the Department of Agriculture. Jeannie at Bousd had an old hen that was 15 years old. There was compensation but that meant nothing to Jeannie.

In the round-up of the ducks, the dairy farm ones in the Village got mixed up with those at the Hotel. That was one big fuss.

Sheep dipping for scab was a police affair. Forms had to be filled in with numbers of sheep to be dipped. The police delegated John MacKinnon, the ferryman, to observe the dipping. He would trundle up on his bicycle. 'If I get the smell of the dip that's all I need,' he would say and sign the form and send it over to the policeman on Tiree on the next boat. ～

Determined not to be disheartened by the failure of his arable experiments Kenneth made a decision that was to become the cornerstone of his farming career. He bought his first pedigree bull at the Perth Sales. It was a Shorthorn and cost 105 guineas.

～ That was a great outing. Hell of a price though. Had him for years. But it was the start to an obsession with bloodlines. I've always been interested in genealogy. I revived the small Highland Cattle fold which was begun by the Estate in 1864 but lapsed during the First World War. The Coll fold was one of the oldest in existence.

No more seaweed from the shore. It was basic slag fertiliser from the mainland that I used. Filthy to work with. Black dust coated the horses as you went along. I was always looking to new methods that would make things more profitable. But then the freight was always a killer.

It wasn't all hard slog. Once a fortnight there would be the respite of the Highlands and Islands Film Guild. Films sent from the mainland were shown in the Village Hall. There were wonderful films. Willie, the shepherd's son, ran the machine and usually got the reels in order. It was a big night out. Everyone went to the pictures. ⁓

But all the while Kenneth and his Factor brother, Carré, were facing up to the fact that the Estate was running at a loss and could no longer survive without financial investment. With an overdraft of £13,000 inherited in 1942 on account of his grandfather's overspend on improvements such as the re-roofing of the Village cottages, a radical decision had to be made.

When Paterson, tenant farmer at Gallanach, decided to leave for a farm near Arrochar on the mainland, the brothers decided not to look for a new tenant but to put it on the market. Gallanach had become very rundown and in need of costly renovation.

This was not straightforward as the whole Estate was entailed which meant that the property could only be passed from father to son or male cousin and never sold, either in part or whole. All the relatives contacted showed no interest. At great expense the entail was broken and the first piece of Stewart land sold was to Kerr Elliot, a farmer with land in Oxfordshire and the Borders.

Despite the very welcome injection of funds to redress the overdraft it was difficult for Kenneth to witness the ease with which Kerr Elliot bought not one but two tractors and flew in by private plane to oversee improvements to Gallanach farmhouse and land.

And so began a period of selling in the late 1950s of not just farms and houses but cottages and ruins, some sold to the first flights of Summer Swallows.

Ironically, the old roofless MacLean castle was sold to a descendant of the very MacLeans from whom the Stewarts had bought the Estate in 1856. The cottages in the village were sold *en bloc* to the tenants for £40 each. There was talk of selling the New Castle for a hotel but nothing came of it. It still stood derelict, a witness to a past chosen to be forgotten by Kenneth.

I think Kenneth would admit it himself; he was not a businessman: 'I was just relieved to sell and get on with the farming.'

Marriage

~~~

Another big event in Kenneth's life was about to take place.

The little girl who had come to the beach parties all those years ago was now a young woman. She and her sister and mother were regular summer visitors, well known to the islanders and to Kenneth's family.

A romance was in the air. Nanny and Patmore were pleased.

Kenneth and Janet were married in London in 1955. It was a family affair at St Michael's in Chester Square. The reception was at the nearby flat of Lady Monckton, Janet's aunt. The night before the wedding there was a dance at Grosvenor House.

The honeymooners toured in Italy and France. I can't help but think the groom was as interested in the rural landscape he passed through as he undoubtedly was in the sights and views he and his bride saw as they wandered along the Left Bank and through the Uffizi Gallery in Florence.

Looking at the photographs of the time they record a

young man relaxed, a million miles away from the hard existence and challenge that had become his lot on a remote Hebridean island.

～ Yes, those few occasions in my adult life when I was in London reminded me of what I could have been. Sometimes I regret the fact that I went to Coll at all.

All my cousins went into the City. They never had a life like mine. They commuted from the Counties to London offices on the Brain Train, rushed back with work to do at home.

It might have been rather nice to have a life like that. Did they envy me? I think they appreciated the fact that I only had enough to buy stamps . . .

You see, I had no peer group on the island. I'd inherited the Laird thing. But I was just a farmer, really. Tiree was a crofting island. Their Laird was the Duke of Argyll. He didn't live there. In Mull they were 'Summer Lairds' with business interests in the south that funded everything.

Janet was a brave woman in coming to Coll. 'Great all together!' That was the height of acclaim on Coll, that saying. ～

On returning to the island the ferry crew were given a bottle of whisky for bringing the bride safely home and there was a big sit-down meal and dance in the Village Hall in the evening. The islanders had subscribed to a fund for new kitchen furniture for Acha, which would be the newlyweds' home, Dorothy having moved to the Lodge which had originally been the Factor's house. Acha was no different from the other old houses on the estate; the gift for the kitchen was much needed and appreciated.

~ There was a list of contributors detailing how much each family had given – 2/-, 10/6, £5. Just like they did for Show funds and still do to this day. For everyone to see. There was great rivalry between Friesland and Cliad for that kind of thing. Cliad got a tractor before Friesland. That started a war.

Katie Coinneach who lived at Hill Cottage gave Janet an embroidered apron. She had no legs or arms, just a funny little foot. She was an amazing character. Had a treadle sewing machine that she worked with that foot. I was touched by that gift.

It was very much an island event with rather a lot of whisky. Lachie Ballard kept his tobacco in his mouth as he ate his dinner and the visiting telephone engineer played the accordion. There were a lot of speeches. ~

Thus began a marriage that has stood the test of the calms and tempests of island time. A suitable metaphor for a sea-girt partnership. Both individuals are strong and independent characters. For more than fifty years their love of Coll has been the linchpin of a lasting friendship that has overridden all the difficulties.

Janet learned to cope with a way of life that was very different from her home life in the south of England. Holidays are one thing but to live in a remote and declining islanded community took grit and stamina and, for all her diminutive size, she had plenty of both.

A deluge of Government pamphlets and news items had started to draw attention to the problems of the depopulating areas of the Highlands and Islands: *Highland Opportunities: A Guide to the different kinds of Assistance that can be attained for Agriculture, Fisheries, Forestry and Industry.* Lengthy articles in the *Oban Times* and *Glasgow Herald* had headlines like *Revitalising Land of the Clearances* and *Argyll's Population Survey Depressing.* One of Janet's self-appointed new roles as helpmeet to her husband was to write prolific letters over all the years of their residency on Coll to the newspapers, national and local, demanding responses from the authorities to the scandalously inadequate services provided to the island.

Kenneth and Janet were also helping to raise the population. Fiona was born in 1956, Fenella three years later in '59 and Nicola in '63.

The West of Scotland Agricultural College keenly promoted new ventures for island farmers. The Hebridean Bulb Growers Ltd was created and Tiree and Uist took part in the production of daffodil and tulip bulbs, not flowers, for the Dutch market.

~ Kerr Elliot was the first to try on Coll. Against my instincts, I planted thousands of bulbs at Arileod. Good sandy fields they were. I appointed Lachie, who had been king gardener in the Castle days, as manager. Thought he would like that.

In August the 'Bulb Girls', mostly students, would come for the lifting. They stayed in the old school in the village that Elliot had turned into a hostel. They livened the place up. They came to work in the back of Duncan's trailer. He was the manager at Gallanach farm. We had some dances there during those summers.

But Lachie got fed up. 'It's not gardening,' he said. 'It's not farming,' I said. And I was the beggar that was paying for it. The tulips never did. They got tulip fire. Flowers rotted. Disease spread by the wind. Another disaster. Those ruddy bulbs nearly put us out of commission.

That's when I decided it would be better to get back to cattle and sheep and forget all the new-fangled ideas. ∾

These were relentless years committed to the annual cycle of hard graft.

∾ But I remember one holiday spent in one of Nursie Pursie's caravans in the East End at the back end of the year in October. I never slept a night in any other place on Coll. It was for the girls' sake. They loved it. People thought we were mad. ∾

* * *

Kenneth's workforce of eight consisted of older islanders who had not been tempted away to the bright lights of Oban and beyond. He advertised for farm workers with young families. Deserted farmhouses like Totronald and Kilbride were once again inhabited, albeit with resident lodgers behind the wood-lined walls. Rats. I know this for a fact for we were one of the young families.

Our coming to the island was fired by my early impressions. Where better to bring up a family protected from the Swing of the '60s? It was called running away from the rat race. (How ironic! The ones at Totronald did not have bowler hats, however.)

We were part of a wave of young people, scattered throughout the islands, who wanted to break away from the conventional pattern that our parents had knitted for us. Oil lamps, water hauled up in buckets from the well, no boat for days on end in the winter. All the boxes were ticked; the very things that the islanders did *not* want.

For the most part Kenneth tolerated us but I think he saw us as romantic amateurs no matter how focused, passionate and hardworking we undoubtedly were. He knew his islanders of old and their hopes for electricity, running water and a decent pier. We, however, revelled in the last of the 'old ways'.

* * *

The Highlands and Islands Development Board was created in 1965 with the specific brief of stemming the depopulation of the region. Once again committees consisting of government officials, scientists and sociologists toured the islands. More drams in lots of village halls.

Dr Iain Skewis and Mr Prophet Smith were very keen on encouraging fishing on Coll and grants were available for new boats. Tourism and small businesses were on the agenda also.

~ If you asked for £50,000 for tourism or business you got it on a plate. If you asked for £5,000 for cattle troughs, not a penny. They were not interested in farming. ~

This is when Janet came into her own. She had always been willing to help out on the farm and had done her stint at filling the corn sheet at sowing time in the early days. And, of course, the letters.

The birth and upbringing of their three daughters had then taken up most of her time. Nannies and *au pairs* like myself saw how she (and we!) coped with that dour old peat-burning Rayburn at Acha, the mud and dung-covered boots, jackets and dogs in the porch, the erratic water supply from the burn that stained the new bath brown and was too peaty to drink, necessitating a walk to the well with buckets for drinking and cooking water each morning. Gas lighting was supplemented by oil and Tilley lamps that had their morning ritual of paraffin filling and wick trimming.

After the birth of their third and last child Janet took over the running of the Village shop on the death of Cathie MacLean's husband, Ian. She cleared out the old store and made it into Coll's first cafe. Up above, the rooms were made into self-catering flats. Out the back, the original corrugated-iron extension built for Gordon Fotheringham, Clerk to the Estate, and his growing family of six children, was made into a self-catering chalet.

In time she did up other properties for holiday lets: Breachacha farmhouse and Bothy, the Garden House and Stronvar, the wooden chalet by Breachacha beach built in 1934 for the shooting guests of Kenneth's grandfather. Janet was determined to contribute to the family fortunes.

Which were still precarious.

* * *

The HIDB initiative, with its promises of help to small island communities like Coll and Tiree, stirred up local action. There was no opposition when Kenneth put his name up as one of the Parish District Councillors for the two islands.

∽ At last there was to be a meeting about the gas and coal. Everyone turned up at the hall. Michael Noble, our MP and Secretary of State, was there. A friendly man. He farmed in Argyll and knew the scene.

The Hydro Electricity Board announced that they had made a great deal for us with the Calor Gas Co. The Hydro would subsidise Calor Gas to give us cheap gas.

We'd had a lot of trouble with inferior coal deliveries on the puffer boat and it must have been on Arthur Nundy's mind. He stood up and addressed the presiding table. 'We asked for coal and you give us stones. We asked for electricity and you give us gas.'

Michael Noble, endeavouring to keep control at the Council Meeting, asked for the next item on the agenda. Callum Salum from Tiree shuffled his papers (which were kept in the deep litter system, he said). Determined to get the point across on our behalf, for Tiree had had diesel-generated electricity for 20 years, Callum Salum said, 'Mr Noble, the people on Coll want to know when they are going to see the light.' They had humour those old boys.

The next plea was for a pier. Not much hope there. In our archives there is a plan for a deep-water pier dating back to 1879!

I happened to meet Michael Noble in Oban later. I'd heard that Craignure on Mull had had the go ahead for a new pier. I'd also heard that a County Councillor had said, 'Those people on Coll don't really think they are going to get a pier?' 'Yes, we do!' I said. 'We're entitled as much as Craignure.'

I think things got moving after that.

Michael Noble surely pushed buttons somewhere for we got both eventually. The pier came first but the electricity came more than ten years later. ∽

* * *

The Seaman's Strike of 1966 further underlined the precariousness of island living. It was a national strike and lasted from 16 May to 1 July. A state of emergency was declared and Navy boats brought supplies to the larger islands with piers. Alistair Oliphant, the hotelkeeper on Coll, ran the ferryboat to Tobermory on Mull twice a week for the essential bread. But most serious was the lack of mail and newspapers, Coll having no air service at that time. As the strike went on supplies from Mull became limited and the fishery protection vessel *Letterston* made it to Coll with flour, potatoes, bread and fuel. The meticulously planned naval manoeuvre to all the smaller islands was called 'Operation Shortbread'.

The Beginning of the Rare Breeds

~

Kerr Elliot had decided to sell Gallanach and then out of the skies, literally, flew a Dutchman, Jan de Vries. Wealthy foreigners were buying land in Scotland with a view to latter day 'lairding' as well as investment. And so de Vries bought Gallanach.

He then approached Kenneth. He was keen on acquiring more land on Coll to establish a shooting estate. His chequebook was big. Kenneth was reluctant at the beginning of discussions for de Vries was not content with just a couple of thousand acres; he wanted substantially more. Eventually in 1965 the five tenant farms of Cliad, Lonban, Kilbride, Friesland and Grishipoll were sold to de Vries – a total of 14,000 acres. It was agreed that Kenneth would rent back Kilbride for grazing.

De Vries was a prosperous international businessman. The Lodge (Dorothy had died in 1965) returned to the grandeur of its origins: crateloads of pheasants were imported and a helicopter was permanently parked in the yard at the back of the coalree. A gamekeeper, gardener and housekeeper were employed and Kenneth witnessed the re-enactment of the pursuits and patronage of his grandfather so many years ago.

～ Had to live with it. It was not a good relationship latterly. The day Dr de Vries signed for the property of the Lodge in November '65 my mother died in Fife at Strathmiglo so the Lodge had been sold with her as a sitting tenant and therefore it went for half the asking price. ～

Financially freer overall, however, Kenneth could now focus on the farm, not only rearing store cattle and sheep but also concentrating on studied breeding programmes.

～ I was an early member of the Rare Breeds Survival Trust. I crossed Blackface sheep with Leicesters. Had 300 of them in the Tomb's field. Then I bought Suffolks; they produced lots of twins. I built a lambing shed. After I got involved with the Trust I had far too many sheep, I admit – 2,500 in the end. But that was much later.

The Department of Agriculture came in with lessons on machine clipping. Diesel generators, of course. I hated the machines. Got contractors in – everyone did. I much preferred the hand clipping but they were long, sweating and swearing days.

That Shorthorn bull was producing pure Shorthorn cross Highland calves. I was a founder member of the Luing Cattle Society developed by the Cadzow brothers.

We still cut hay. Then this wonderful stuff called silage appeared on the horizon. We were no longer weather dependent for winter fodder. It didn't matter if it rained. But dry days still made better silage. ～

The new pier was started in 1964. A road had to be built first from the village to deeper water on the way to Caolas-an-Eilean. At a cost of £178,000 it was finished in 1967.

∿ They took long enough about building that pier but there were not many men on the squad. They lived in huts at the bottom of the hill.

Don't know how much whisky they drank in the process but they made a good job of it. The wee foreman was permanently drunk. That was when Donald Stornoway came to the island. He ended up marrying Wee Morag and staying. We always said the cement was mixed with whisky not water. ∿

There was a resounding cheer when Captain Gunn and the *Claymore* came alongside and tied up at the pier for the first time. Shortly afterwards a dinner dance was held in the Village Hall to celebrate the auspicious occasion.

It is not difficult to imagine what a revolutionary change the new pier made. No more swamped journeys out in the ferryboat, no more transfer of cars, cattle, sheep, mail and supplies from the *Claymore* by hoist, rope and sling. To say nothing of passengers. No more black winter mornings waiting on the jetty to see her lights come round Caolas-an-Eilean, not knowing whether one would get aboard or not.

∿ That was the beginning of an easier life getting stock on and off the island. Bigger boats came, like the *Loch Carron*, which could carry 700 tons of cargo, and the *Loch Ard* which could take all of 500 tons. She had an enormous crane structure but MacBrayne's preferred the *Loch Carron*. The two of them came from Glasgow and did week about.

Then it was the car ferries for stock. At sale time they came specially. No cars as there were so many complaints from car owners about the mess. But passengers could go. Different now. I think the cars come first.

Stirling became the new market. I stuck with Oban. Being Vice Chairman at Corson's I was involved with modernising the Mart. And I got called the Laird of the Loos, again.

Everything got so much better.

And that was when I really got involved in rare breeds. ⌒

The Rare Breeds Society was founded in 1972. Kenneth had finally found his mission in life. He started with Jacob sheep. The men in the Mart in Oban had never seen such creatures and thought they were goats.

Then came Hebrideans, Manx Loughtons, Shetlands, Herdwicks, Shropshires, Oxfords, Portlands, White-faced Woodlands, Rylands, Borerays, North Ronaldsays. The Soay tup was a favourite. It had been hand reared as its mother had died at birth and was very tame compared to its cousins from the far-flung archipelago.

There were 72 breeds registered with the Rare Breeds Society at that time. Kenneth had 55 of them.

'There's an awful lot of coming and wenting,' the Captain of the *Columba* observed, as the panoply of unusual animals went to Oban – and came back.

But it was not the same animals coming back; the Coll stock *had* been sold at the Rare Breeds Show in Stoneleigh in Warwickshire and Kenneth was bringing back *more* . . .

Stoneleigh is the highlight of the Rare Breeds year.

Trailers never came back to Coll empty from that market, much to Janet's concern – though her holiday tenants at Stronvar in the Castle field were delighted. The West End became a veritable Noah's ark of endangered farm animals. Cattle were included in the passion: Highlanders, Luings, Blue Greys, Galloways and Shetlands. The ancient breed of Longhorns wandered across Breachacha beach:

∼ 'Everyone's got them now . . . ' ∼

Reputed to have the largest collection of rare breeds in Scotland, Kenneth was asked to judge the Ryland Sheep at the Highland Show in Edinburgh and became the first chairman of the Hebridean Sheep Society when it was formed in the late 1970s. He also judged Primitive Sheep in York.

All the while commercial farming still had to be the backbone to his 'hobby', as some saw it. It was still difficult to attract workers from the mainland but the Day of the Big Switch On was nigh. In 1979 the whole island lit up to almost louder cheers than at the opening of the new pier.

∼ We were told by the Hydro in 1970 that there was little likelihood of us getting any electricity for another ten years. Well, they delivered with a year in hand. Give them that.

Cables were laid from Tiree. Everyone wanted to be connected. I think it was £1,000 per household.

Our then MP Mr Ian MacCormack came for the Big Switch On ceremony at the Hotel. Whole island turned up. Afterwards it was like first footing at New Year. People went round each other's houses to see them lit up. In Fox's tiny wee sitting room you were blinded by a 150-watt bulb.

Boatloads of freezers came in. Flora at Arileod became the Queen of Electric Gadgets. The electric carving knife the *pièce de resistance*.

For myself the wall heater in the bathroom was ultimate luxury. No more paraffin heaters.

Best of all were the lights in the steadings and sheds. Especially at 6am on a winter morning. ⌇

Move to the Borders

~⁀

Life should have been getting easier but Kenneth's enthusiasm ('addiction', his family would have said) for his
beloved rare breeds was taking over his life and all his
fields. As any specialist breeder knows the lure of creating
the definitive bloodline takes time and space. At 55 years
old he was still working a full day with a small workforce
and would not let up. That was the pattern, the habit of a
lifetime so ingrained, for the next ten years.

Who knows what the catalyst was but on 31 May 1989
Kenneth suffered a stroke as he walked beasts by the New
Castle, his ancestral home.

Months of mainland rehabilitation could not give him
back the use of his left arm and leg.

In 1991 the decision was made reluctantly to sell up the
last of the Estate and retire to the mainland. With only
five acres of Borders soil, Janet felt confident that a couple
of fields for a few of his favourite rare sheep would keep
Kenneth happily occupied.

Soon neighbouring and far-flung fields were being

rented to accommodate expanding numbers of sheep and cattle. This was a difficult and stubborn time. Declining mobility ultimately made him accept that his involvement with his treasured rare breeds was now in the well deserved and rewarding role of nationally respected figurehead of the Rare Breeds Society.

To the advantage of Coll, which can sometimes be critical of its fortunes, good and bad, it had been decided to sell the property in lots. A whole new generation of incomers came to the island. Now there are many lairds, big and wee.

Janet and daughter Fenella retained Stronvar, the General's chalet for 'the Shooters' of long ago and now long favoured holiday let. Guests can look out over Breachacha beach to the castles, Old and New, both now permanent homes of resident islanders, and muse on times past.

Since 1991 Kenneth has only been back to Coll on two occasions. Family and friends bring back the latest stories from the island. The Last Laird listens keenly and mulls them over before adding them to his storehouse of memories. Visiting him one is aware of his enjoyment of a new kind of bloodline: that of his reminiscences of Coll, which are to be shared and passed on to generations to come.

⤳ You know, there was a calf that was last in its bloodline that I sold with all the other stock at the selling up of the Estate when we were leaving. I bought it back to take to the Borders. ⤳

The General's Last Word

~⁓

It seems appropriate that the stories and views of one man's life on a particular Hebridean island should include the words of another, his grandfather, who in his own way wrestled with similar challenges on Coll.

The following letter was published in *The Scotsman* of 1 July 1937.

Decline in Population
Western Isles of Scotland
Case of Coll and Tiree

Brigadier General E.M.P. Stewart writes from Breachacha Castle, Isle of Coll

The recent enquiry conducted by Sir John Sutherland as chairman of the Scottish Development Council has adduced such strong evidence of increasing decline in population that their clamant needs can no longer brook delay.

Taking the linked islands of Coll and Tiree, provided by nature with soils of great fertility and perennial verdure, the decline of the population affords striking proof of the urgent need of attention and definite action on the part of the Government. At the present time there are approximately only 272 persons on Coll and only 1,400 on Tiree, as compared with 1,442 and 5,000 respectively a little less than a hundred years ago.

Danger of Becoming Derelict

Unless this rapid decline, symptomatic of almost all the Western Isles, is arrested, and immediate remedial measure applied, these islands will become derelict, Coll approximately in 1970, Tiree in 2000, within two generations.

There comes an earlier stage, however, which cannot be too strongly stressed, where the community in each island can no longer carry on.

It is evident that a minimum number of officials is required for the well-being of every community, e.g. postmaster and staff, medical officer, minister, school teacher, ferrymen, hotelkeeper, factor, storekeeper, police etc., their families and assistants. So far as Coll is concerned, the minimum is estimated to be 40 to 45 persons; hence if the present rate of decline, 8 per cent to 10 per cent, continues, Coll will qualify for evacuation about 1964, that is in less than one generation from now. The same applies with equal force to Tiree, and doubtless to other of the Western Isles.

It is a fearful fate abhorrent to the islanders that demands deep and serious consideration.

The First Remedies

Regarding the land – as population declines, rats, rabbits and other vermin, bracken, noxious weeds, deterioration of soil and drainage increase at an alarming rate and extent. Therefore, as long as labour is inadequate, government grants and concessions have little value toward restoration of fertility and resuscitation of agriculture and people.

It is the root of the problem that needs immediate attention. The prime remedy for Coll is a substantial pier, agitated for since 1879. Next the establishment of a vocational training centre, with a demonstration farm for youth.

To this end I am prepared to offer facilities in feus and leases of land etc.

Another important matter is a great reduction in freights or subsidised freights on all essential foodstuffs, agricultural equipment and fertilisers for all the islands.

The general drift of the younger generation to the mainland must be arrested lest the islands become derelict.

* * *

But Kenneth himself must be allowed to have the very last word on Coll.

∼ I never could understand that announcement on the boat. 'Thank you for travelling with Caledonian Mac-Brayne.' How else would we get there? ∼

Life on Coll

~~~

After many taping sessions with Kenneth I realised that, given the vast quantity of material and the tantalising tangents taken, not everything he said could be interwoven with the story of his life. Momentum would be lost.

Hence this addendum, where I have grouped together various topics which otherwise might not have not been saved to print.

Island Connections

Anyone living on an island knows how dependent they are on 'the boat'. In Kenneth's time there were many; from steamships to the latest RoRo car ferries. But always that link by the mercy of the weather.

For the most part we have a regular and reliable service, but as I write the boat has passed and will not call today, winds of 70 miles per hour chasing her back to Oban. At least two Collachs are trapped aboard, one returning from hospital. There is a wagon of building materials for

75

a new house and accompanying workforce. The emptied domestic oil supply lorry is stranded on the pier and the hotel keeper has returned to his hotel with his bare refrigerated trailer to await calmer conditions for the very necessary supply trip to the mainland. Being the winter timetable the boat will not come to Coll for a further two days. Weather permitting.

The cattle and sheep sales are past, thankfully, but there have been times when stock was aboard that did that round trip and didn't have a B&B or friends to stay with back in Oban. It is equally frustrating for the farmers when the stock are meant to be leaving the island for a sale. Missed sale, missed income and winter feed starting to run out.

Imagine the situation before the new pier when the boat anchored in the bay and the ferryman had to judge conditions before setting off from the jetty in the village to tie up alongside. Passengers, mail, supplies and sometimes animals handed up to the open side door before the reverse procedure.

I have my own memories of travelling in that ferryboat. Seven months pregnant with our second child, I was going to Oban for a check-up. It was to be a family outing but by the time we got alongside the *Claymore* the weather suddenly turned nasty. Being a bit awkward in size I was pulled up first by the crew at the open side door while the Captain was yelling down from the bridge 'Get back! Get back!' to Guy, the ferryman. With the increasing height of the waves the ferryboat gunwale was in danger of being trapped under the belting of the hull of the bigger boat and tipping everyone overboard. I made my way up to the bridge to see the ferryboat heading back to the jetty, husband and two-year-old wanly waving. There was no cajoling Captain Gunn to wait for another try. 'Look, lassie, they'll be lucky if they get back to shore.' They did. And I went on to Oban for a very solitary outing.

For transporting of stock a cargo boat would come but it was the same method. Kenneth and his men singly handing up 1,500 lambs on one occasion. Individual cows were winched aboard on a sling round their bellies. They swung like pendulums over the water.

~ 'Why don't you come into the pier?' This was always the great cry in those days. 'I will,' said old Captain Lachie Ross of the *Clydesdale*, 'if you put another stone on the end, I'll come.' They were great characters those skippers. Amazing skills. How they managed in bad weather in open bridges.

The *Hebrides*, older than the *Clydesdale*, was a black old thing. Stokers and coal and the racket of her winch. On the go from the 1890s. One high tide Donald MacFarlane, her skipper, took her right to the pier. We could walk the cattle straight onto the deck. If the authorities knew he would have got hell.

Wartime lunch on the *Hebrides* was a fine affair but maybe not available for the airmen going to Tiree: hot roast beef or cold roast mutton then stewed prunes or figs or apples with semolina or ground rice pudding. I was always amused. When did you get hot roast mutton or cold roast beef? I didn't have the courage to ask. The saloon was at the stern of the boat and you ate with the officers. Everything was rationed. 'And do you all take sugar in your tea?' the steward would ask. 'A spoonful each in your cup, that's it.' No bowl on the table.

When the *Hebrides* came in the summer there was a piano on the deck and locals boarded and joined the tourists in dancing eightsome reels. It was 'MacBrayne's Time'. Eventually the ropes would be cast off and hopefully all the locals back on dry land.

Once Captain MacFarlane was chatting with a tourist up on the bridge while waiting for the ferryboat to come alongside. 'Coll is very bleak looking,' observed the tourist, 'just rock and heather.' Just like they say today. Looking down into the ferryboat as she tied up, filled with cheeses up to the gunwales, he was amazed. 'Golly! Cheese! Where the hell do they get that?'

'Oh,' replied Captain MacFarlane, 'it just grows on bushes on Coll.'

* * *

You could sleep on the boat in Oban before she left in the morning. The *Iona* had cabins on the top deck. Climbing down the steps in a gale was not easy. They were not cheap so I would economise and book a berth. You had to share.

I had met a couple of old Barra crofters in the Royal Hotel after an Oban sale. One of them regaled us with the condition of his ulcer. Could only drink milk straight from the 'freedge', he told us. Blow me, the old boy was on the boat that night in the bunk below. He talked half the night. He only took his boots off. Heat rises when you are in the top bunk.

One night I slept in the crew's mess room. The steward came in periodically and gave me a cup of tea. Very pleasant.

The cargo boat usually came on a Saturday afternoon. It was either the *Loch Carron* or the *Loch Ard*. But it was 'MacBrayne's Time' again. By arrangement, the purser would phone either Sarah, John Allan's mother or Peggy Neillach, Neilly John's mother, from Tobermory with time of arrival on Coll. The boat got later and later in turning up and the two old ladies in turn would yell down the phone with dog's abuse. 'Bloody disgrace sending boats at this time of night,' shouted Sarah, or the equivalent, for she had hardly a word of English. You see, after a day's work the men on the island were still needed to unload the cargo and get it delivered.

The purser got the message – whether Gaelic speaking or not.

If the cargo boat came on a Sunday because of weather or breakdown there was all hell let loose. Letters of outrage sent to the manager in Oban. 'But we cannae *never* send a boat to Coll on a Sunday . . .' he protested.

The ferryboat was always a two hander – one to steer, the other to man the engine which was amidships. And both to handle the ropes, though there was always someone to help at that. John Allan and Neilly John were the team for many years with 'Captain' Davy Fotheringham at the ready.

And then there was Guy Jardine, the ex-hotel-keeper and one of the ferrymen when John Allan had to retire. A sling of stobs burst over the ferryboat and John Allan's back was damaged. Guy was a character. Always the kilt though sometimes shorts in the summer. The boat was in the bay. Tups were coming back from a sale but the crew got the Coll tups mixed up with the Tiree ones. In the confusion a couple fell into the sea. Add to that the overfull sling of supplies for the shop shifted as it came over the ferryboat and Sproat's boxes of sausages were seen floating over to Caolas-an-Eilean.

Wee John MacKinnon, the Tiree captain, shouted down from the bridge, 'Never mind the tups! Get Sproat's sausages!'

On the way back to the pier Guy was seen to be leaning over the gunwale of the ferryboat. Over he went, kilt and all. Clambering back onto the ferryboat he said it was his pipe that had fallen over the side. Had to get it. 'Aye,' said Callum, 'they say his pipe was still in his mouth when he went over.'

It must have been about the same time. For whatever reason I was part of the ferryboat crew. Bob Petrie was at the engine; Alistair Oliphant at the bow rope. The two of them were the joint owners of the Hotel. And I steered alongside the mail boat, believe it or not. I managed to throw the stern rope but Alistair had the bow rope knotted at the bow and couldn't let it go. So I released the stern rope and we swung round 180 degrees and hit the other side of the boat. The Captain was yelling blue murder.

∽ 'Three men in a boat – two hotelkeepers and a farmer.'

* * *

It was not funny when the cow got killed. With the new pier built it was much easier to load cattle onto the new car ferries. No winches, no slings. They were walked onto the car platform of the *Columba* which could face sideways, tide permitting, onto the pier. Down they went on the lift and into pens in the hold.

A terrible thing happened in Oban when this poor old cow was left to wander about in the hold. Next time the lift came down she was crushed to pulp. They tried to hush it up. Cruelty people in Oban went to town. Quite right.

It is all much better for the beasts nowadays; they have to travel in closed trailers driven onto the RoRo ramps. But that is how it was. Changed days.

But everyone still goes down to the boat when she comes in and when she goes out even although cars just roll on and off its backside these days. ∽

* * *

Planes never helped with the shipping of cattle and sheep but they became an important factor in the well-being of communities in remote locations. Captain David Barclay was the co-founder of the Scottish Air Ambulance Service in 1933. The De Havilland Rapide was the plane with which he saved many lives by getting patients to mainland hospitals in time. His first mercy flight was to evacuate a seriously ill fisherman from a beach on Islay. Possibly his second mission was to another beach. On Coll.

~ The first time I saw a plane land on Breachacha beach was in 1934 when Johnny Claic's toes were blown off by the Shooters at Cornaig Lodge in the East End. The doctor in the Village had to go to Mr Sturgeon at the post office to phone the mainland for help. There were only three phones at that time – the Keeper, the Castle and Sturgeon's. All wind-up jobs.

Johnny was flown in that first ambulance plane to the Southern General in Glasgow. He came back home to an awed hero's welcome in the East End.

One of the pilots had a crush on one of the secretaries in the Castle. My grandfather had secretaries that typed endless letters to the papers and his military contemporaries. Landing on the beach was always hazardous. Wind and tide. One of the planes got bogged in the quicksand by the Old Castle. Maybe it was the spooning pilot not concentrating. Two of the farm horses had to pull it out.

Landing strips were built when BEA took over the contract and also provided scheduled domestic flights. So did Loganair later. Feall plain was used in the beginning but Totronald and Ballard finally favoured. An army of soldiers camped at Totronald and levelled the strips. Ballard was too short.

There was always trouble with cows and horses at Totronald. I'd get a message at work to say that a plane was coming in and to clear the runway. It wasn't possible to drop everything, just like that. The pilot would be left circling, cows running in all directions. My blood would boil if they were due to calve.

A plane crash-landed at Totronald once. A collapsed wheel. Pilot and passengers were fine but later on when it was decided what to do with the damaged plane, what a job we had moving it to the tank landing craft waiting on Breachacha beach.

We had to put it on a sledge we'd built that was higher than the fences. It was towed along the road, wings hanging over the fields. It took five tractors to pull it up Totronald brae. When we got to the beach hawsers were attached to the plane from the landing craft but we still had to help manoeuvre it over the sand with the tractors. A hawser slipped. We all got bogged.

Throughout it all I remember the ship's Commander sending some of his crew off to fill bags with sand for his children's sand pit. He came from the south of England. ∼

* * *

After many years without air service, save emergency ambulance plane or helicopter, Coll now has a regular plane on Mondays and Wednesdays to and from Oban with connection to Tiree and dedicated weekend 'scholar' flights for the secondary pupils at Oban High School. The plane is a nine-seater Islander. Our current pilot is called Captain Angel. She lends a propitious air to the journey. Unfortunately (though it's only unfortunate in this context), there are many more than nine secondary school pupils, but a pattern has evolved. Some take to the skies, others prefer the wider social space of the CalMac boat even although travelling time is so very much longer.

Games and Celebrations

The Tobermory Games is a well-marked date in the calendar, not just for Mullachs but for people from all over the world. Sadly the days are gone when a special sailing was laid on by MacBrayne's for Coll and Tiree folk to enjoy and participate and imbibe in the events of the gala day. The Coll children were drilled all winter at Chrissie MacKinnon's Highland dancing class. 'The following will volunteer', as they say in the army. But she was good. Many silver cups and shields sat on Coll mantelpieces the following winter.

It was also a chance to meet up with friends and family from Tiree and Mull, go to the rebel outpost of the Clydesdale Bank where kind-hearted manager Angus MacIntyre always had the answer to financial problems, shop in the Co-op and, best of all, go to Brown's Ironmongers where the proverbial feather duster to an anchor could be bought. And the butcher's always on the list.

⌒ I never went. I knew I would maybe imbibe too much. Sometimes I was the ferryman collecting the staggering bodies coming back off the boat returning from Tobermory, the entire ferryboat crew being the most unsteady of all.

Neilly John had been to the butcher's in Tobermory and treated himself to a pound of liver which he stuffed into his shirt pocket. On the boat coming back at the end of a very hot day, he and Sturgeon got into an argument. No doubt to do with the lobsters and the best place for the creels, etc, for the two of them worked a boat over at the back of Arileod. It never came to fisticuffs but tourists looking on became very concerned. Neilly John's chest was covered in blood.

I hoped the holidaymakers on the boat had got the right story. ∼

* * *

Concerts, dances and the Coll Show were occasions, like the Tobermory Games, when islanders gathered *en fête* – and still do. The Village school, now Talla Lan, was the venue before the hall was built. Badminton was played in the school, which had a well-sprung wooden floor. It was the time for East and West to meet.

Everyone wore their best. At concerts Iza Irvine from Crossapol played violin and sang with a floating lacy handkerchief tied to her wrist. The men were smart in suits and ties, the ties crumpled into pockets by the end of the night. Perfumes wove in and around the vapours of whisky once the dancing started.

∼ I wore a kilt on those occasions. My father's and grandfather's as a little boy, my great-uncle Charlie Stewart's as an adult.

At dances all the men would be standing up round the fire at the beginning of the night and the women seated on the chairs and benches along the wall. There were no toilets – women out of the back door, men out of the front. You took your own drink. If you wanted a drink at the hotel beforehand it was the lean-to shed with a window through the wall and jam jars to drink out of. I liked a drink but I was never a pub person.

Davy Fotheringham played the squeezebox. He played better the more he drank. And if you could get her to play, Gracie Cranaig, Davy's sister, played piano. She had a special stool to sit on as she had one leg shorter than the other. Angus Arinthluic played pipes for the Eightsome Reel. But it wasn't all Highland dances. The quadrilles were great. But very complicated. In and out and round about and then you galloped round the room with your partner. We zoomed round. They don't do them now.

Janet loved the tango, which she danced with Willie, the shepherd's son.

Hughie Broadhills ordered bread for sandwiches and five dozen boxes of cakes from the mainland for concerts and dances. He was nicknamed the Duke as he was the only child in the West End to have boots in the days of the Acha school. The rest of the children walked over the hill barefoot. He started delivering bread and cakes round the island in a pony and trap pulled by a white gelding called Roger. I'd go with him when I was younger and collect the boxes from the boat marked Beattie's Milanda Bread and Cakes. You could get two kinds of bread – plain with thick crusts, black toasted on top and golden on the bottom. Sliced or unsliced. Pan loaves had soft crusts all round and were a bit more posh.

* * *

A dance was held for my twenty-first birthday. There was a barrel of beer set up in the back porch of the school. In the clear up next day there was Davy lying under the barrel catching the last drips and still playing the squeezebox.

Good fun we had at those dances, you know. ⁓

The 'Glasgow bread' still comes to the island but not in such quantities these days. Many islanders make their own, whether with a breadmaker or oven. But in those days not every household had an oven and girdle scones were more customary fare. Those with ovens however baked just as traditionally, if they could afford to – oven scones, gingerbread, Dundee cake, black bun, etc. So when entrepreneurial Hughie introduced sweet mainland bakery delights there was no going back. A doctor at the time believed this development and the coming of electricity contributed to 'the depression' that became the lot of several of the older women of the island. Many traditional chores were diminished and time hung heavy.

But not when it came to Show Day. Farmers and their womenfolk rallied to show off their best in horses, cattle, sheep, dogs, poultry, horticulture, knitting – and 'the baking'. When I was first asked if I did 'the bakin'' I thought I was being tested on my culinary skills with pork.

⁓ The Coll Agricultural and Horticultural Show was inaugurated in 1880 by John Lorne Stewart. Everyone had to participate. It was stopped during the First World War but was revived in 1936 or '37 at the original site at Cliad where it stayed for a couple of years until it went up to the dairy in the Village and finally by the hall at the Lodge.

That first Show Day after the Great War there was a big dinner in the granary that was above the byre at the Hotel. I climbed up a ladder at the back and looked in at the long tables covered in white tablecloths and all the great and the good sitting round.

People went to great lengths to win cups. The best I heard was the ploy that Sturgeon's son, Robert, and John Thompson, the Factor's son, got up to. One of the hens to be shown had the wrong coloured legs for the breed. They were yellow instead of black. With Zebrite, stuff for blackening stoves, they rubbed her legs black. Don't know if they won a prize or not. But whatever those two got up to they did a great deal for the Show to keep it going.

At Show time a Miss Murchie came to the island and with other 'hen wives' from the College gave talks on poultry and butter making, in the school as well as at meetings.

They did away with the horses at the Show years and years ago. Then the cattle. Think it is only sheep now. And vegetables. ∼

Livestock classes are greatly reduced at the Show these days but the tables of vegetables, baking, crafts and children's produce are never big enough and the day not long enough to see and, more importantly, hear everything that is going on.

The General would be pleased at the category for 'Arrangement of Coll Flowers or Grasses in a Bowl or Vase' but confused, I think, at the baking section which lists 'Cherry Cake MEN ONLY 3lbs'. What he would have made of 'The Best Shaved and Polished Head to be judged at the Dance' is anyone's guess.

***

Funerals were another occasion when everyone was expected to get together, for less celebratory, but equally thirst-quenching reasons. There are two graveyards on the island. One mid-island at Killionaig, the other at Crossapol at the end of a mile-long beach to the south. Both are a long walk from the Village, more so the latter. In the days before motorised transport *uisge-beatha* was a very necessary 'water of life' for mourners going to the graveyard after the church service. Women were not allowed to go to the graveyard.

～ The funeral procession to the graveyard was led by a sort of Master of Ceremonies. Everyone followed in twos behind. The coffin was at the end carried by six men, three on each side. If the family had money it was made of shiny wood; ordinary wood covered with a black cloth if they were poor. Every so often the MC would call out '*Cuir Stad!*' meaning halt or stop. This was the signal for a rest and change over of the coffin carriers. They'd have a dram and a bit cheese. The instruction to get going again would be issued and six men from the front would stand to the side of the road until the coffin reached them and they would take over the carrying.

At Uig on the way to Crossapol there is a big stone that was a traditional resting place. It is about six miles from the Village. The thirst was keen by then. '*Cuir Stad!*' came the command and after an appropriate recharging of body and soul the cortege set off once more. Half an hour later and halfway to Crossapol someone realised that the coffin was not with them.

It had been left high on the bank of grass by the big stone at Uig.

Shows how many people there must have been at that funeral.

At least there was a road to travel on most of the way. To both graveyards. Going cross country from Arinthluic to get to the road you were up to your waist in the bog. Some job for the coffin carriers. We did fall back – and down – more than once.

What a whiff came off some coffins. ～

Beliefs and Superstitions

Kenneth paid a customary respect to both churches on the island but it was possibly conditioned by his early religious experience with his grandfather at the Castle.

The Church of Scotland was the Established Church, the 'Lairds' Church'. It is now called the High Church – not on account of any rarefied doctrine but rather because of its elevated position above the Village. The majority of islanders in Kenneth's early life attended the Wee Free Church further down the hill.

It is a reflection of a very changed society on Coll that the Free Church windows are all boarded up these days. Funerals, weddings, christenings and weekly services are held in the High Church for all denominations and the church also becomes the venue for concerts and school prize givings.

~ I only went to the Free Church for funerals. It seemed to me whatever you did you had committed some sin. Everything you did was wrong. I was terrified of Free Church ministers when I was young. But there was a nice wee FP* minister when we first came to live on Coll. Even my grandfather liked him.

Mr John Robertson, a minister from Skye, was not approved of by my grandfather. Ironically he was Church of Scotland. They were all sorts, the ministers. He preached doom with a capital D but I know now he was being very topical. 'That black cloud that hangs over us – the atomic bomb . . .' I didn't know what he was talking about. I'd never heard of an atomic bomb.

* Free Presbyterian

Over the years we had many ministers and mission-
aries. For both churches. There was one who was ob-
sessed with drink. Got everyone to sign the pledge. Even
Neilly John signed. I refused.

When I was working the farm all hours of the day
and night I would get exasperated at Free Church
Communion time. Services started on a Wednesday
through to Sunday. Thursday was Fast Day when there
were two long, drawn-out sermons. One morning, one
evening. Everyone the length of the island just stopped
work and downed tools. It wouldn't matter if it was
beautiful weather for harvesting during that period.

There was a visiting minister who, in between the
two services on the Fast Day, went for an afternoon
walk. 'What were you doing treading the Lord's Day
underfoot?' the elders asked at night. 'There's nothing
about not going for a walk in the Bible,' the minister
replied. The elders had their reply. 'Maybe He did it in
the Holy Land, but He wouldn't get away with it here.'

After the war there was an evangelical movement,
Tell Scotland, with Billy Graham. He didn't come to
Coll himself but some of his followers did. They were
accommodated at the Hotel. When Mrs MacQuarrie,
'Ma Ma' as she was known, presented the bill she
was told God would pay – i.e. send the invoice to the
Glasgow office. 'God pay for me, too,' said the Pakistani
salesman who always slept in the kitchen on 'the settee',
which was a car seat. ∽

* * *

With the decline in indigenous islanders so too the telling
of old Coll stories is dying out. This book will, I hope,
make amends. New islanders are creating their own
storylines and the young are too absorbed in the stories on
their Facebooks.

Place names are changing. Grishipol on the north side is now known as Greesh. Affectionately, but it is disturbing. Undray corner is the Hungry corner to some. Will it be a matter of time before the tale will be told of the impoverished family that died there of starvation during the Clearances? Mysterious lights used to be seen at that corner at night. Car drivers would wait in the lay-by for the oncoming vehicle to pass. It never came. Nobody sees 'the lights' today.

~ The islanders were terribly superstitious and wouldn't talk to the likes of me on the subject of second sight.

Sproat's wife's family were known to have 'the gift'. If Big Archie looked over the end of the pier it meant a body was coming back. Meaning there would be an island-related death on the mainland. His sister, Katie Sproat, would sometimes be found standing on the pier long after the boat had gone for no reason. She is said to have walked along the shore to where the new pier would in time be built and just stand looking out to sea. When the pier was built the first coffin to be brought back to the island was the first since the old pier days.

A story told to me by the old folks concerned an old Collach who lived in a tiny cottage near Ballard. The ruin is there to the left of the gate. This is before the First World War. A mother and her wee boy came to visit the old woman, who touched his fair curly hair. 'What a pity,' she said, 'his hair will be in the seaweed.' The boy grew up and went to the mainland. He came back on holiday and said he was going fishing off the rocks over the back of Arileod between there and Totronald. He didn't come back. A search party went out. His body was found on the rocks, his head covered in seaweed.

And here's another one. Some fishermen from the East End went off for a day's fishing but did not come back that night. Or the next. Many more nights passed without sign of them. Everyone gathered at the cottage of an old woman who had the second sight. She went out the door and lifted a stone and counted the slaters (wood lice) underneath. They totalled the number of men. 'They'll be back,' she said.

One day their sail came over the horizon. 'It's God's will that brought you all back to us,' the family and neighbours praised. They had been blown onto the uninhabited side of Rum and been stranded there for a fortnight. 'Aye, that may be,' said one of the older fisherman, 'but we did a wee bit ourselves.'

John Ballyhaugh said that if he ate a swan's egg there would be an addition to the family. There were always lots of swans and cygnets on Ballyhaugh loch. Well, John did have a big family.

* * *

The older people on Coll told me many times about the Brahan Seer's prediction that the last Laird of Coll would be called Cionneach – Kenneth. Some of them had the book about the Seer in their house. Apparently he had said the last Laird would be lame and have no male children. Well, that's true.

* * *

The Brahan Seer was burned alive in a barrel of tar and pushed over a cliff. Quite right. ∿

Postscript Revelations

It can now be told that the mythical island of Struay where a certain character called Katie Morag lives is not a million sea miles away from Coll. A house here, a beach there and the row of whitewashed cottages in the Village by the old jetty of the ferryboat days are recognisably Coll. Nowadays the word 'ferry' translates into floating cafeteria and car park. Katie Morag and Grannie Island would find the concept most disturbing.

Study the map of Struay and you will find that the indent of Village Bay is the only topographic similarity to Coll. Scattered about are a few local place names but further study will show that the majority are stolen from neighbouring islands and parts of the mainland personal to me. There are several references to Powell and Pressburger's *I Know Where I'm Going* which was filmed on Mull in 1945. The mountain range called the Five Sisters of Struay have their mainland counterpart in Kintail. In fact their illustration is inspired by neighbouring Rum, the nearest to mountains that Coll will ever get.

Katie Morag is thirty years old and her long-ago birth in *Katie Morag Delivers the Mail* was a nostalgic self-indulgence on my part, celebrating our young family times on Coll in the 1960s and '70s. Collachs of that time I have illustrated in the early books: Guy Jardine with his pipe and kilt (the one I thought was the Laird), Neilly John with the crack in his bum showing above his always slipping down trousers, Mrs Campbell and her greenhouse at the Roundhouse and the much claimed Grannie Island. Some say she is Janet's mother but I know she is an amalgam of my own hopes of the grandmother I wanted to be and Grannie Spencer, a redoubtable woman on Mull who ferried supplies to her island during the Seaman's Strike in 1966. And anyway, Katie Morag's grandmother was meant to be a grandfather called Grinpa. But that is another story.

Over the years other islanders have crept into the illustrations but if you look closely you will sometimes see a man with a donkey jacket and a faded skip bunnet standing on the jetty.